A GIRL
CALLED RED

JADE MARIE

authorHOUSE®

AuthorHouse™
1663 Liberty Drive
Bloomington, IN 47403
www.authorhouse.com
Phone: 1-800-839-8640

Published by AuthorHouse   12/08/2014

ISBN: 978-1-4969-4638-6 (sc)
ISBN: 978-1-4969-4637-9 (e)

Library of Congress Control Number: 2014918130

Any people depicted in stock imagery provided by Thinkstock are models,
and such images are being used for illustrative purposes only.
Certain stock imagery © Thinkstock.

This book is printed on acid-free paper.

Because of the dynamic nature of the Internet, any web addresses or links contained in
this book may have changed since publication and may no longer be valid. The views
expressed in this work are solely those of the author and do not necessarily reflect the
views of the publisher, and the publisher hereby disclaims any responsibility for them.

This is a work of fiction. All of the characters, names, incidents, organizations, and dialogue
in this novel are either the products of the author's imagination or are used fictitiously.

This book is dedicated to my son, Jayden and
also to the victims of cyberbullying.

People may not remember exactly what you did, or what you said, but they will always remember how you made them feel.
—Maya Angelo

ACKNOWLEDGMENTS

I would first like to thank God for giving me the vision to write such an inspirational novel.

Secondly, I want to thank my son, Jayden, for showing patience while I was working on this project. I hope that one day you can read this book and understand why I spent so much time in front of my computer.

To my family, thank you for being patient with me during the process of me writing my novel and also for being so understanding about the temporary absence of quality time spent with you all.

I would like to send a special shout out to my siblings, Terrance Wright, Rondall Barnes, Blake Brown and DeShawna Barnes. Although we may not talk every day on the phone, I just want you all to know that I love you more than words can ever express.

A big thank you to Ivious Barnes, Sureda Lucas, Brittany Young, Bernice Wright Muhammad, Leotis Holiday III and Kevin Jr. for listening to all of my crazy ideas. I would have probably given up on writing if it wasn't for your encouraging words.

Thank you, Jacquez Howard (@mintgold) for all of your encouraging and kind words throughout my writing process. Whenever I felt like taking a break or simply giving up on my book, you were there to give me the extra push that I needed in order to continue on and for that I will be forever grateful to have you as a friend. May God continue to bless you and your clothing line, *Mint Gold*, now and in the future.

Miss Gabriel Moore, aka. Gabriel Cashmere, thank you for your kind words, being that you were one of the first persons that I told about my novel. May God continue to bless you, your family and your passion for writing.

I would like to express my gratitude to Mrs. Rose E. Marshall, Jacqueline O'Dell, Skylet J. Lucker and Riquita Anderson for critiquing my work and genuinely seeing me through this book.

I would also like to send a special shout out to John Sams (@stayfocused26), thank you for all of your kind words of encouragement. Also to DeMario Taylor for assisting me with the first poem in my book, titled "No One Love's You, Not Even You".

Thanks to my publisher, AuthorHouse, for encouraging and guiding me throughout my writing process.

I would like to thank Karen Stansbury for assisting me during my publisher's, selection process.

Thanks to my editor, the design team and all of the technical reviewers who worked on this book, not only for catching my mistakes, but also for taking the time to perfect them.

Last and not least, I beg forgiveness of those names I have forgotten to mention, who have also supported me over the course of me writing my novel.

INTRODUCTION

Beep ... beep ... beep ... was all I heard when I came to on April 26, 2012. I rose up with the anticipation to stop my alarm clock from beeping but instead found myself attached to several IVs and a heart monitor. Unfortunately for me, the beeping noise wasn't going to stop anytime soon, nor was the shouting that came from my parents and loved ones.

"She's up! She's up!" my mother shouted.

"Go get the nurse!" another voice summoned.

After lying back against the hospital bed, I began to feel my body go into shock from all of the commotion that was taking place in the small room. Not to mention the excruciating pain that I was enduring at that very moment—from my aching stomach and throbbing headache, it seemed as if someone had hit me over the head with a frying pan.

When the nurse finally entered the room, she immediately began to check my vitals while cautiously avoiding the stitches that ran across my left wrist. Then it hit me. "Damn! I'm still here," I said to myself. After taking over more than a dozen of my mother's prescribed sleeping pills and slitting my wrist, I was still alive.

The emotions that took over my body were at first overwhelming as some of my loved ones planted kisses and gentle hugs amongst my weakened body. The reason being is that it was an unfamiliar feeling that I had longed for since I was a small child—called affection. But without any warning, the atmosphere quickly turned bitter as my subconscious mind asked, *So this is what it took for you to get a little attention from your family—or anyone else for that matter?*

My mother must had felt my resentment because she immediately loosened up her grip from around my shoulders. As tears filled her eyes, she began to ask me over and over again, "Why, Trinity? What would make you want to end your own life?" Before I could answer my mother's question, my father escorted her out of the room while telling her before they were completely out of sight that now was not the time.

CHAPTER ONE
UGLY DUCKLING

Five months prior to my incident, my reflection stared disturbingly back at me from the opposite side of the mirror, watching as I struggled to pull my hair up into a ponytail. "Finally," I said to myself while snapping a couple of clips into my hair to help secure the naps.

"Trinity, hurry up in there!" SJ yelled while banging on the other side of the door.

"Hold your horses!" I yelled back. Having lost track of time, I hadn't realized that I had been locked in the bathroom, which I shared with my siblings, for nearly an hour. Ignoring my brother's request to use the bathroom, I continued to examine myself in front of the long mirror that hung behind the bathroom door.

There I stood at five foot three with a skin complexion so pale that everyone confused me as being a young Caucasian woman. That is, until they laid eyes on my large nostrils and red bushy hair. You see, when I was born, my father gave me the nickname of Red because of my ginger-colored hair. But my birth name is Trinity Haynes.

Despite my petite frame and pearly white teeth, I would often stop smiling whenever someone stared at me for longer than usual because of my bad skin. It seemed as though when one pimple disappeared, five would reappear out of nowhere. There wasn't any Proactiv or any other deep-cleansing products that could prevent my embarrassing breakouts. My dermatologist had informed my parents and me years prior that the breakouts were caused by an imbalance within my hormones and that they would eventually balance themselves out later on during my life. It just didn't seem fair that I had been cursed with the bad hair and skin, along with all of the other unappealing traits, while my siblings on the other hand were lucky enough to inherit all of the gorgeous ones. Unfortunately for myself, no matter how many times I blinked in front of the mirror, wishing to switch bodies with my older sister, Raven, it was official that I remained an ugly duckling.

Raven was the eldest of my parents' children and unlike me, she was very stunning. Everywhere we went, people complimented her on her beauty and fashion. She stood at five seven with a beautiful, caramel complexion that complemented her gray eyes. Quite the opposite of mine, she had the type of nose that many paid to have, small and pointed. Along with the dark and soft textured hair, that hung down to the middle of her back. Being the social butterfly that she was, she was chosen to be the captain of our high school, cheerleading squad. During her free time when she wasn't cheering or gossiping on the phone with her friends, she would spend the remainder of her time with her boyfriend named, Seth Rogers. I often resented their relationship because it left me with no one to talk to other than my cousin named, Michelle.

Last but not least was my kid brother, SJ, who was named after our father, Steven. Not only was he named after our father, he was also a spitting image of him, with his caramel complexion and curly, black hair. My brother's athletic frame stood at five eight, which often gave him and his teammates the upper advantage in every sport that they played in at his junior high school. Similar to my sister's social life, he too was very popular around his school for his charming looks and athletic skills. In which both qualities often led to him being chastised by our mother, whenever she got word about a love letter that had been intercepted by one of his school teachers.

Chapter Two

GUESS WHO

~~~⌘~~~

It was a cold and gloomy day in Savannah, Georgia, when my family and I all gathered around the dinner table to listen as my Uncle Hank blessed the food that had been prepared for our Thanksgiving dinner. After grace was said, it was traditional for my family and I to go around the room and share with everyone what we were thankful for. While some shared how they were thankful for their careers, finances, and great health, I always shared how thankful I was to be surrounded by such a loving family, despite of my grandparents' absence. I believe that my family and I would have been more concerned if my mother's parents had actually shown up to our family dinner, on the count of my grandfather disowning my mother after he discovered that she had been knocked up by a black man.

My grandfather's name was Ray Earl Jennings. He was born and raised in the suburbs outside of Vidalia, Georgia, where he had a reputation around town for being a former member of the Ku Klux Klan. Although my siblings and I had never met him in person, we often overheard some of the horrible stories that our mother shared with our father behind closed doors.

Despite of her husband's wishes, my Grandmother Martha Jennings, however, secretly kept in touch with my mother through my Uncle Hank and Aunt Karla. She made it her personal business to make an appearance at my parents' wedding and also at the hospital for all three births of her grandchildren. I guess the saying *a mother's love is unconditional* was really true because regardless of what color her son-in-law and grandchildren's skin were, she was there to support my mother when it mattered the most.

Other than those few times, the only time we ever heard from my grandmother was when she sent out her yearly holiday cards that sometimes contained money for my siblings and me. As much as we wanted to show our appreciation for the cards and money, we were told to never reply to any of the letters because it would've been just her luck if our grandfather had decided to check the mailbox and recognized any of our names on the envelope.

"Let's eat!" my Grandfather Curtis yelled out after carving the turkey. We then took turns digging into the turkey, pasta salads, macaroni and cheese, dressing, yams, greens, and glazed ham that covered our dining room table.

While everyone was busy stuffing their faces, my father sat at the head of our dinner table, bragging about our newly remodeled basement that he had completed just in time for the holiday. Since it was my family's turn to host Thanksgiving dinner that year, he had gone out and purchased some new appliances just so that he could show them off to everyone who attended the dinner.

My father was a very intelligent man and within six years of graduating from law school, he made partner at his law firm. Not only did he have a reputation around town for being intelligent, but he was also known for being good looking. I had to admit that for my father to be in his early forties that he didn't look half bad for his age. Although his skin complexion was a couple of shades darker than my siblings, my mother was just as much in love with him today as she was when she first laid eyes on him nearly twenty years ago.

Sitting next to her knight in shining armor, was my mother, Kelly Haynes, who was also known as the former Miss Savannah. Before she and my father married, she competed in multiple beauty pageants throughout the country. But shortly after giving birth to my sister Raven, she decided to trade in her high heels for a pair of gym shoes. Which led her to her new career as the Physical Education teacher and the assistant cheerleading coach at my brother's middle school. For as long as I could remember, she had always been obsessed with her health and fitness. Luckily for my family, my father and brother did majority of the cooking because otherwise we'd be forced to drink protein shakes and eat salads every night for dinner.

"So, Karla! When will the family have the opportunity to meet this 'mystery man' of yours?" My mother asked my aunt, who was sitting across the table from her.

"Oh, I don't know, Kelly. You know that I'm not big on rushing things when it comes to relationships," my aunt replied.

But as usual, my mother saw right through my aunt. After all, they were identical twin sisters and also best friends. Before the two of them had begun adding their own additions to their families, they were practically inseparable. Whenever the two of them got together, they would share some of their childhood memories with my siblings and me, regarding some of the "switch-a-roo" pranks they played on my grandparents and their teachers throughout their school years.

I had to admit that from afar it was sometimes difficult even for me to tell them apart because they looked identical and they both wore their hair in the same short hairstyle. Luckily for my mother, she had a birthmark on her arm that helped distinguish the two of them whenever it came time for my aunt to be punished by my grandfather when they were growing up.

My Aunt Karla was a recently divorced, ex-housewife who was currently living off of her alimony. In which I may add, that she wasn't doing half bad for her not to have worked a single day in her life. My aunt was married for ten years to one of the top-paid architects in Savannah, before they finally decided to call it quits. Rumor has it that my uncle at the time was having an affair with his high school sweetheart named Daisy Dixon, who he later married after he and my aunt's divorce was final. But before the two of them walked away from their marriage, they agreed to share joint custody of their twelve-year-old son, Jacob, and their four-year-old daughter, Emma. During the weeks that my younger cousins were away with their father, my aunt and her new lover would take lavishing trips out of town.

"What mystery man?" my Uncle Hank asked, butting into my mother and aunt's conversation. "The only man you need in your love life, Karla, is the man above," he said while pointing towards the sky. My Uncle Hank was my mother and aunt's younger brother and also the assistant pastor at our church. After my grandfather's decision to disown my mother from their family, he and my mother grew extremely close. Despite their racial upbringing, he accepted my mother and her extended family with open arms, regardless of our skin color. My family and me always enjoyed having him and his wife, Jennifer, over to our house, especially my mother because my uncle's presence often helped to fill the void in my mother's heart that my grandfather had left there. No matter what time of the day it was, he was always there for my family even though he had his wife and their golden retriever named, Louie to attend to back home.

Before I could hear my aunt's reply, I received a text message from my cousin, Michael who was sitting at the other end of our dinner table with his parents. "It's time!" the message read. Michael Khalif Kyles, who preferred to be called Michelle instead, was my best friend and also my cousin. When he and his family first moved back to Savannah from California, he would tease me and my siblings for having such a deep southern accent and in retaliation, we would make fun of the way that he dressed, from his preppy attire on down to his penny loafers. But after having a few tea parties and dressing up in some of my mother's old clothing, the two of us grew very fond of each other.

Being that he was the only child, Michael spent most of his time over at my parents' house so that my siblings and I could keep him company. As the years went by, he shared with me how he felt that deep down inside, he should have been born as a girl. To make him feel better about himself, I too shared with him about how difficult it was for me to fit in with others being that I didn't know if I needed to act more black than white or more white than black.

Although we were both struggling with our identities and self-esteem, he and I shared a special bond that no one could break. To prove it, we both snuck and got matching lotus flower tattoos on our ankles, using the fake IDs that Michelle's ex-boyfriend had gotten made for us.

After being excused from the table, Michelle followed me up to my bedroom where he immediately changed out of his cardigan sweater and fitted jeans into his red dress and knee-high, leather boots.

I knew at that moment that it was time for our plan to be put on display. Regardless of whether I was ready or not, Michelle was determined to reveal his darkest secret to the people that he loved the most.

"How do I look?" she asked after applying the finishing touches of makeup to her face. As much as I hated to admit it, Michelle looked better as a female than I did, especially with her long, curly wig that I had helped her put on.

"You look absolutely amazing!" I replied while passing her the letter that I had helped her write to her parents, which read:

To my dearest parents,

I'm writing this letter to let both of you know that I love you with all of my heart. But I can't let another day go by without being true to myself or my lover. Over these past few years, I've tried to convince myself on numerous occasions that I would someday marry one of the most beautiful women here in Savannah and that we would live happily ever after in a big house with a white picket fence. But unfortunately, that dream will never come true for me, being that my lover is a man. No matter how hard I've tried to hide, prevent, or erase these feelings, I simply cannot. I want you both to understand that true love doesn't have a face, color or gender. No matter what happens from here on out, my love for you both will always be unconditional. If the two of you no longer want to claim me, I totally understand. I've saved enough money from my job at Pizza World for me to be emancipated so that I can possibly still live my fairytale life with or without your approval.

Love Always,
Michelle

Before Michelle and I joined the others in the family room, I took her by the hand to give her the reassurance that I was going to support her no matter what the outcome was.

When we finally reunited with the others, we found that they were playing a family game called *Guess Who? What perfect timing,* I thought to myself as I cleared my throat and extended my hand out toward Michelle's direction.

"Guess who?" I asked while watching nearly everyone in the room, mouths drop open. The room went from being full of laughter and chatter to complete silence. I could tell just by looking at the expressions on everyone's faces that they were either disturbed or in shock.

"What in the hell is going on here, Michael?" Michelle's father asked while rising up from our living room sofa. "Is this some type of sick joke?" he asked while burning a hole into Michelle's pupils.

Before Michelle was able to answer any of her father's questions, the ex-pro football player, attempted to charge her with all of his might. "Fred, no!" My Aunt Lena shouted out, as the rest of the men in the room cut his charge short. Too frightened to speak, Michelle dropped his letter onto his weeping mother's lap before making his way out of our front door.

Chapter Three

DON'T BE TARDY FOR THE PARTY

"Shorty got them Apple Bottom Jeans,
boots with the fur, with the fur,
the whole club was looking at her,
she hit the floor ... ♫♫♫"

My phone sang, before I answered, "Hello?"

"Good morning, Red! Where are you? Everyone's waiting for you," Michelle said. It had been nearly three months since Michelle had come out of the closet, and being that she was her parent's only child, my Aunt Lena pleaded for her husband to allow for Michelle to continue living under the same roof as them. But my uncle, being the stubborn man that he was, was very hard to bargain with. It was either his way or no way—that is, until my aunt threatened to move out of the house, taking Michelle with her. Not wanting to jeopardize their marriage, my Uncle Fred quickly gave in under the conditions that Michelle had to dress like a boy while living under his roof.

"I'm still in bed," I replied.

"So are you not attending the meeting for your parents' surprise anniversary party?" she asked.

"Omg! It totally slipped my mind! What time is it?" I asked while rubbing my eyes.

"It's 12:30 and everyone's here except for you," she replied.

"Okay, I'm on my way!" I said before disconnecting the call and jumping out of bed.

It was a quarter till two when I finally joined the others at my grandparents' home. "Help yourself, Red" my grandfather said while extending his hand out toward the brunch that my grandmother and Aunt Lena had prepared for everyone.

"I will, thank you!" I replied while joining Michelle and the others at the dining room table.

After spending nearly an hour or so going over the menu, decorations and the agenda for my parents' surprise dinner, our meeting was finally adjourned.

Since my siblings and their friends were responsible for decorating the venue, Michelle and I were in charge of notifying each person on my parents' guest list that had RSVPd. After calling the forty-ninth name on the list, there was one more call that had to be made.

"What are you waiting for?" Michelle asked.

"Shhh … keep quiet," I said as the other end of the phone rang.

"Chalmers' residence!" the soft, voice said from the other end of the telephone.

"Good afternoon, Mrs. Chalmers! This is Kelly and Steven's daughter, Red—I mean Trinity. I was calling to remind you and your family that my parents' surprise party will begin at six o'clock sharp next Saturday evening," I responded nervously.

"Thanks for the reminder, dear. We'll definitely be there!" she replied.

"Okay, great, I'll see you then!" I said before ending the call. Although my ten-second conversation with my future mother-in-law seemed like a ten-minute conversation. My heart continued to race, knowing that my lifelong crush named, Ian Chalmers was going to be in my presence at my parents' surprise dinner.

"See, that wasn't so bad, now was it?" Michelle asked with a disturbing expression on her face, as I pounced around my bedroom in circles, pretending I was waltzing with Ian.

"No, it wasn't, but now I have to find something to wear," I said while grabbing my car keys from off of my vanity and making my way out of my bedroom door.

"Wait for me!" Michelle yelled while following close behind me.

CHAPTER FOUR

GIOVANNI'S

"Hello! Is there anything in particular that I can assist you two with today?" a raspy voice asked from behind the register.

"Hi, Sammy! I didn't know that you worked here," Michelle said while holding up a red dress against herself as she admired herself in the mirror.

"Yeah, I work here part-time to help my mother out with the place," Samantha replied. She was a former classmate of ours before she graduated and took on her new role as the assistant manager, at her mother's clothing boutique.

After informing Samantha that I was in search of an evening gown, she brought out some of the dresses that had just been delivered to her boutique that morning. There was a nice selection to choose from, but since I had a bad sense of fashion, I allowed Michelle to select a few options for me.

The first dress that I tried on was too short, the second was too large, but the third one fitted me just perfectly. "What about this one?" I asked while modeling the burgundy, halter dress in front of the large mirror near the dressing room.

"It's perfect! From the color to the design, you've finally found something that complements that red hair of yours" Michelle replied jokingly.

After going back into the dressing room to remove the knee-high dress, I stared off into the mirror while daydreaming that Ian and I were slow dancing together at my parents' surprise dinner. As I closed my eyes and began to spin myself around in a circle, I was interrupted by a knock on the door. "Are you okay in there? You've been in there for over twenty minutes now," Michelle complained.

"I'm coming, I'm coming!" I shot back with an attitude.

"Well, hurry up! I'm starving out here," Michelle ranted. After spending nearly all of my allowance on my new dress, Michelle suggested that we eat at her boyfriend's restaurant.

Giovanni's was an Italian restaurant located in the suburbs of Savannah, and being that Michelle's boyfriend was the assistant manager, we ate there quite often. On our way over to the restaurant, Michelle sent her boyfriend a text message to inform him that we would be stopping in to have dinner.

When we entered the restaurant, Michelle and I were immediately greeted by one of the hostess. "Good evening, Michelle! Table for two?" the waitress asked.

"Yes, please," Michelle answered as the waitress escorted us to our table.

After placing our beverage orders, we then debated on which entrées we were going to try out on that particular day. That is until Michelle got distracted from gawking at her lover. I had to admit that Michelle's boyfriend was pretty hot. With his tanned complexion and dark hair, he looked as though he had stepped fresh out of a Calvin Klein ad. Catching Michelle's gaze from across the room, the slender man immediately began to blush.

"What can I get for you two on this lovely evening?" a deep Italian voice asked.

"Hi, De Angelo! I'll be having my usual, please," I replied.

"And for you, Miss?" he asked while looking at Michelle.

"I think I'll try your daily special," Michelle shyly replied.

"Okay, one chicken Alfredo with a Caesar salad and a shrimp penne dinner coming right up," he confirmed before walking away from our table.

"Can you believe that he's only seventeen and is already running this place?" Michelle asked while admiring her lover from a far.

"Yeah, he's definitely a keeper!" I replied, giving her a wink.

Michelle definitely had something to brag about, being that her lover graduated early from high school at the top of his class. Which he later moved back to Savannah from New York, to help his uncle out at his restaurant.

"Hey look! There's your parents!" Michelle said, while waving to my parents who were seated across the room from us. I looked up in surprise, not just because it was my parents, but because I was surprised to see my mother actually eating at Giovanni's, on the count of her not being too fond of Italian food.

Moments after Michelle had spotted my parents, they both stood up to put their coats on. "I wonder where they're running off to in such a hurry" I said aloud as my father made his way over to our dinner table.

"How's it going, you two?" my father asked.

"Hey, Dad! Everything's going just fine, but where did Mom go?" I asked, concerned.

"Oh, your mother went to warm up the car," he replied nervously while offering to cover our dinner tab.

Not wanting to con my own father, I simply declined his offer, while ignoring Michelle's hand gestures from behind-- telling me to keep quiet about our meal being free.

"Okay, well in that case I'll see you at home," my father said before making his way out of the restaurant.

"Well, that was awkward." Michelle said, as we watched the two of them drive off from the restaurant.

Chapter Five
RED LIGHT SPECIAL

After Michelle and I ate dinner, we headed over to her place so that I could drop her off at home. "Not again." I said as we approached a red light that always took an extremely long time to change.

"Oh snap! This is my jam!" Michelle said while turning up one of Whitney Houston's greatest hits to the max.

"Share my life, take me for what I am ..." Michelle sang while cueing for me to join in whenever the backup singers would sing. As I followed Michelle's lead, I closed my eyes and pretended to be one of Whitney's backup singers. Which back fired on me because I had totally forgotten that we were sitting at a red light. That is, until the cars behind me started to honk their horns.

When I finally reopened my eyes, I noticed in the car next to me, sat Ian and a couple of his friends from the football team, who were all laughing and pointing in my direction. As I lowered my imaginary microphone away from my mouth, I quickly sped off towards the direction of Michelle's home to avoid from being humiliated any further.

"Are you okay?" Michelle asked as I pulled up into my aunt and uncle's driveway.

"Of course not," I said while putting my head down against my steering wheel.

"Everything will be okay," she said, assuring me that the group of boys would probably forget all about my performance by the time Monday came around.

* * *

When I had finally made it home, I ran into my mother in the kitchen, who was scavenging around in our refrigerator for something to eat.

"Hey, sweetie! What do you have in your doggy bag?" she asked while pointing at my leftovers from Giovanni's.

"Oh, just some pasta and a couple of breadsticks," I replied.

"Ugh, I'll pass. You already know how much I dislike Italian food," she said, with a look of disgust on her face.

"But you were just—"

Ring, ring, ring! My mother's phone sounded before I could finish my sentence.

"Sorry, honey, I have to take this call," she said.

"But you were just at Giovanni's," I said under my breath as I watched her leave the kitchen.

Chapter Six

IT'S YOUR ANNIVERSARY!

"Okay, everyone, they're here!" my sister announced as everyone quickly took their places in the large party room. My parents' surprise anniversary dinner was being held at Jasmine Gardens. Which was a very popular establishment in our city where individuals hosted elegant events, such as proms, receptions, *quinceañeras*, and much more. Luckily for my parents, my grandparents had reserved the building nearly a year in advance.

As the others waited silently for the countdown, I quickly scanned the room hoping to see Ian's face in the crowd, but unfortunately he was nowhere in sight. The feeling was bittersweet because I had practically spent my entire life savings on my new makeover for someone who barely even knew that I existed. "Don't let him ruin your night," I said to myself while trying not to let the disappointment show on my face.

"Surprise!" everyone shouted after my grandfather silently counted down using his fingers. The expressions on my parents' faces were priceless as my mother's eyes filled with tears of joy. She and my father had been under the impression that my Aunt Lena had made reservations for the two of them at an upscale Jazz restaurant, where my father's favorite Jazz band would be playing. But to their surprise, all of their family and friends had gathered in celebration of their crystal anniversary.

While my parents were being showered with hugs and kisses, Michelle and I decided to branch off from everyone so that we could admire some of the breathtaking decorations that filled the room.

There were inflated balloons, flashing lights, crystal chandeliers and mini ice sculptures everywhere. Along with a photo projector that displayed several photos of me and my family throughout the years. "Wow! SJ and Raven did a fantastic job with decorating the place," Michelle said in awe.

After taking multiple photos and eating our three-course meals, my parents and some of their guests gathered on the dance floor to dance. As Michelle and I watched the others dance from along the side line, I heard a familiar voice ask, "How's it going, Miss Houston?"

When I turned around to see the person behind the voice, I was immediately at a loss for words. Just his presence alone was enough to knock me off of my feet.

"Ian! We're glad that you could make it," Michelle said while covering for me as I struggled to find my voice.

There I was, finally standing face to face with the guy of my dreams and all I could do was blush. Although I was somewhat still embarrassed from the traffic light incident, I knew that it was now or never for me to engage into my very first conversation with him. But with his glossy, dark brown eyes staring down at me, I just couldn't seem to snap out of the trance that he had me in. Everything about him was intriguing, from the way that he walked, talked and dressed. The red sweater and tan slacks that he had chosen to wear on tonight, complimented his smooth, caramel skin and tall muscular frame to a tee.

Now I know what you're thinking, but so what if I had it bad. He was my eye candy, and with a down to earth personality and swagger such as his, it was nearly impossible for any girl to resist him. Especially whenever he smiled or licked his lips to expose the dimple that was hidden in his left cheek.

"I'm glad that you guys invited me" Ian replied.

"Well, I'm going to leave the two of you here while I go and cut a rug," Michelle said before heading over to the dance floor. "You're not gonna join him?" he asked.

"No, I'll pass."

"And why is that?"

"Because I'm not that good at dancing," I confessed.

"Oh yeah, I forgot that you were a singer instead," Ian said jokingly before his little sister, Veronica came over and escorted him away towards the dance floor.

"What perfect timing," I said to myself as I headed to the ladies' room to freshen up. While I was double-checking my hair and makeup in the mirror, I was joined at the sink by Ian's ex-girlfriend, named Farrah Cummings.

As she sized me up, she informed me that I wasn't Ian's type and instructed for me to back off. "Excuse me?" I asked, with a puzzled expression on my face.

"You're not his type," she said again, but this time a little slower than before. "I've been watching the two of you from across the room, and thank goodness that I sent his little sister over there just in time before you killed him with boredom." She replied.

"I don't know what you're talking about," I said innocently.

"Who do you think you're fooling, Trinity?" Farrah asked, with a firm stare. "I've seen the way you look at him during school, in the halls, and even now," she replied. "Ian wants a girl that he can take home to his mother and show off to his friends, not some unattractive, redheaded loser that can barely hold a decent conversation without blushing like a little girl," she stated before making her way out of the restroom.

As beautiful as I thought I had looked on tonight, Farrah's cruel words had knocked me off of my high horse. *Maybe she's right. Ian would never give a girl like me the time of day,* I thought to myself as I wiped the tears from my eyes.

"There you are! I've been looking everywhere for you," Raven said as she made her way into the ladies' room. "Are you okay?" she asked.

"Yes, my contacts are just a little dry, that's all," I said while trying to keep my composure.

"Okay, well, Mom and Dad are about to cut their cake, so come on out," she said while grabbing ahold of my hand and escorting me back into the party room to join the others.

After eating only a small portion out of my slice of cake, I pretended to have a stomachache just so that I could leave my parents' gathering early.

"Okay, sweetie, go home and get some rest," my father said while giving me a kiss on the cheek.

During my drive home, all I kept hearing in my head was Farrah's voice repeating over and over again about how unattractive and boring I was.

* * *

The following morning, I awakened to several missed calls and text messages from Michelle, all asking if I was okay and why had I left the party without saying good-bye to her. Instead of fibbing to her as I had done to my parents, I decided to be honest with her about my run-in with Farrah the night before. As usual, Michelle assured me that none of the things that Farrah had said were true and that she only targeted me because I was a threat to her. But as much as I wanted to believe what Michelle was telling me was true, I knew that she was only saying those things to cheer me up.

CHAPTER SEVEN
CAMILLA

It was about ten minutes before twelve when I approached my calculus teacher's desk. "Yes, Trinity, you may be excused to use the ladies' room," Mr. Traugott said in his normal, monotone voice.

"Thank you!" I replied as I walked back to my desk to gather my belongings. Being that this was my second year having him as my math teacher, he had quickly caught on to my routinely restroom breaks during my freshman year of having him as my pre-calculus teacher.

After being curious as to why I had always waited until the end of his class to be excused for the ladies room. I quickly responded by telling him that I had a weakened bladder and that it was a must for me to be excused every day during the same time. Although, I was uncertain if he had bought my story or not, he still allowed for me to be excused early each day from his class.

But the truth was that I really didn't have a weak bladder. It was just an excuse that I used to avoid my peers during my lunch period. I considered lunchtime to be long and torturous, being that I had no one to sit with on account of Michelle's lunch period being at a different time than mine.

Since I was normally always the first person in the lunch line, I would quickly grab and stuff my lunch down inside of my backpack before hiding out in one of the stalls in the ladies room. When the coast was clear for me to finally come out, I would then climb up onto the windowsill, before retrieving my chips, a sandwich and my bottled water from out of my backpack.

I had gotten so accustomed to eating alone that it really didn't bother me if I had anyone to talk to or not. That is, up until the moment when I met one of the most compassionate individuals that one could ever meet, named Camilla. She and I had become lunch buddies, ever since she discovered my secret hideout during the beginning of the school year.

Although she stood at only three six, she had the heart of a giant, and there were never enough sticks or stones that anyone could throw to bring down her self-esteem. I admired her in so many ways because regardless of how some people pointed or stared at her for being a little person, she never showed any signs of self-pity.

The more that she and I became acquainted, the more she opened up to me about how she and her family had moved to the United States from Mexico when she was just four years old. Despite of her and her loved ones being separated for nearly eleven years, she would soon be reuniting with them all at her upcoming celebration for her fifteenth birthday.

"How was your parents' surprise dinner?" Camilla asked after joining me in the ladies' room.

"It was absolutely amazing!" I replied, failing to mention my run-in with Farrah.

"Well, I'm glad to know that you all enjoyed yourselves. I wish that I could have made it but being that my family and I have been so busy with prepping for my quinceañara, I just didn't have the time". She stated. "Oh and before I forget, here's your invitation," she said while handing me a pink envelope.

"Thank you!" I replied with a huge smile. There was no way for me to hide my excitement, being that this was the first real invitation that I had ever received from any of my peers.

Chapter Eight

CRAB PARTY

When our lunch period was over, Camilla and I headed to the only class we had together, which was Spanish. Since it was an honors class, the class was filled with mostly juniors and seniors, including Ian. This was my first time seeing him since my parents' dinner, and after my conversation with Farrah, I was too ashamed to even look his way. That is until he decided to take a seat right next to me—on that particular day.

After Ian took his seat, Camilla winked an eye at me from across the room while I on the other hand, turned into putty after I had gotten a whiff of his *Acqua Di Gio* cologne.

"What's up, Trinity?" he asked.

"Who me?" I asked, while pointing to myself.

"Umm yeah, your name is Trinity, right?" he asked with a chuckle.

"Yeah, sorry, you just kind of caught me off guard, that's all," I replied nervously.

"Well, I definitely don't want to do that," he said with a smirk. "I just wanted to tell you that I really enjoyed myself at your parents' anniversary dinner and that I'm still trying to recuperate from all of the dancing that I did that night."

"Yeah, I heard. You must have worn your dancing shoes that night?" I asked while slightly rolling my eyes.

"Something like that," he replied with a little cockiness. "Every time I tried to take a seat, someone would pull me back out onto the dance floor." He replied. "Speaking of which, I tried to save a dance for you but your sister informed me that you had checked out of the dinner early." He stated, while I tried to hide my blushing face.

"*¡Buenas tardes clase!*" the teacher said as she closed her classroom door.

"*¡Buenas tardes!*" everyone replied. Mrs. Garcia was very strict and required for all of her students to speak only Spanish during her class. Whenever one of her students didn't know how to translate an English word into Spanish, she would make them look it up in her English-Spanish dictionary. As she went on with her lecture, Ian passed me a note that read:

Hey! I was thinking that we could get together sometime to have ice cream, if it's okay with you? And btw, I forgot to tell you how beautiful you looked the other night at your parents' anniversary dinner.

Not sure whether I was being punked or not, I quickly wrote my cell phone number down on the note before passing it back to him. Wow, that was fast! I thought to myself as I retrieved my vibrating cell phone from out of my back pocket. But it wasn't Ian who had sent me a text message, it was Michelle instead. "What is it now?" I asked, while opening up the text message that read: *Karma is a b#*@h!*

After reading her text message, I sat back in my chair, clueless as to what type of karma Michelle was referring to. But before I could wonder any longer, a senior named Jennifer Braxton blurted out to the entire class that Farrah Cummings had crabs. As the classroom filled with laughter, Ian quivered in his chair in disgust.

* * *

After the dismissal bell had finally rung, I immediately met Michelle at her locker. "Hey! What in the heck is going on?" I asked.

"I don't know what you're talking about," she said innocently.

"Michelle!" I said in stern tone.

"All right, all right" she said. "Today during me and Farrah's gym class, I snuck into the girls' locker room to sprinkle a little itching powder onto her undergarments."

"You did *what*?" I asked aloud.

"Look, I know what you're thinking, but it was about time someone gave her a taste of her own medicine," she replied.

"So, how did you manage to sneak in without getting caught?" I curiously asked.

"It was a piece of cake," she said. "You see, while everyone was in the pool, I put on my pink hoodie and a wig just before making my way into the locker room, and things just kind of went from there. You should have been there, Red. Everyone in the class, including the gym teacher, watched as Farrah scratched herself uncontrollably before she took off towards the ladies' room," Michelle said while laughing hysterically.

"Listen up, Michelle. Although I know that you were only taking up for me, I want you to understand that your prank was very cruel and on top of that, you could have easily gotten caught." I lectured, while making her promise that she would never go back into the girls' locker room-- ever again.

Chapter Nine
ICE CREAM—PART 1

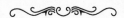

Ian: *Hey beautiful! Wyd*

When I saw Ian's name come across my phone, I nearly fainted as I contemplated on what to reply back.

Me: *Hey handsome! Lol, I'm just sitting at home doing some school work. Wbu?*

Ian: *Not too much, I was trying to see when you wanted to get together to have ice cream?*

Me: *Anytime is fine with me*

Ian: *Ok, cool. Let's do next Wednesday at 6 pm*

Me: *Ok, sounds great!*

Ian: *Alright, I'll ttyl*

After rereading our text messages over and over again, I decided to share the exciting news with Michelle.

Me: *Hey Michelle! Guess who just asked me out on a date?*

Michelle: *Let me guess, President Barack Obama? Lol*

Me: *No, you bird brain … the correct answer is Ian*

Michelle: *OMG Ian? Now this I have to hear. Call me ASAP!*

After having a thirty-minute phone conversation with Michelle that night, I tossed and turned in my bed as I struggled to fall asleep. I don't know what had come over me, as I kept waking up in the middle of the night, checking my phone to see if I had any missed calls or text messages from Ian. "Get ahold of yourself, Trinity" I said to myself, before I was finally able to doze off for the night.

Chapter Ten
ICE CREAM—PART 2

It was a quarter to six when I pulled up outside of Joey's Gelato parlor and as expected, Ian was nowhere in sight. So to kill time, I decided to walk over to the local park so that I could draw a couple of sketches in my sketchbook.

The weather and the scenery couldn't have been any more perfect as I scanned the park in search of something to draw. "Perfect!" I said as I came across an elderly couple that was walking around the park, feeding breadcrumbs to the ducks.

As I began to draw the couple, I couldn't help but to imagine me and Ian's faces on their bodies. The companionship that the two of them shared was everything I had been longing for. From the forehead kisses to the one-on-one conversation that they were engaging in, that left the elderly woman smiling from ear to ear. But right before my imagination could take me any further, I was interrupted by a cold sensation that touched the nap of my neck.

When I turned around, I found Ian standing over me, holding a large, pistachio gelato in one hand and a medium, raspberry one in the other. "What do you have there?" he asked, looking down at my somewhat finished masterpiece.

"Oh just a drawing," I replied modestly, while closing my sketchbook.

"Nice work!" he said while handing me my treat.

"Thank you! But how did you know to get me a raspberry-flavored gelato?" I asked.

"Well, correct me if I'm wrong but I figured that it was your favorite being that you often apply the same flavored gloss to your lips each day during our Spanish class," he replied while waiting for me to confirm if his hypothesis was correct.

"Correct, you are!" I replied shyly. There wasn't anything that he said or did that didn't seem to amaze me.

"So while I have you here, I wanted to know if you would be willing to tutor me in calculus and also in Spanish," he said, with his hypnotizing eyes once again staring down at me. With his charming looks and genuine personality, how could I possibly turn him down? After all, this was probably going to be my only shot at spending any quality time with him, so why not take advantage of it, I thought to myself.

After agreeing that I would tutor him, I received a phone call from my father, who was questioning my where abouts being that I was running late for dinner. "Sorry, Dad! I totally lost track of time, but I'll be home shortly," I replied while quickly gathering my belongings. "Thanks for the ice cream but I have to go." I said to Ian as he walked me over to my car.

"No, thank you!" he replied while handing me his math and Spanish folders from out of his father's old-school Camaro. "You don't know how much this means to me. My coach told me that if I didn't get my grades up that I wouldn't be able to play in the championship game next month." He stated before promising me that he would call me later on that night.

CHAPTER ELEVEN
DOUBLE LOSER

"Raven, may you please pass the Ranch?" I asked that evening as my family and I all sat around our dinner table, feasting on the garden salad and chicken enchiladas that my father and brother had prepared for everyone. Unlike your typical family, my family and I all ate dinner together at least twice a week so that my parents were able to keep up with everyone's busy lives.

"So, how's school going for everyone?" my father asked while looking up at me and my siblings.

"School's okay with the exception of me scoring nearly thirty points during my last basketball game!" my brother announced.

"Well, that's great, son! But let's try putting just a little more effort into your schoolwork as you do your sports," my father replied.

"Yes, sir," SJ said, staring down at his plate.

"Well for me, school is going just as planned. I made all A's this semester with the exception of my prom and graduation soon approaching and I finally got my acceptance letter from Spelman College today in the mail!" My sister gloated as my father raised a toast to acknowledge her accomplishments. While everyone was in such a good mood, my sister took advantage of the moment by asking for my parent's permission to attend her prom with her boyfriend of two years.

"Well, I don't see why not. After all, you two have been dating for quite some time now and Seth really does seem like the perfect gentleman," my mother said while looking over at my father for his approval.

"And how's everything going with you, Red?" my father asked.

"Sure, why not!" he added.

"Nothing too exciting other than me making the principal's list again," I replied.

"Well, that's great, honey! Keep up the great work," my parents both replied.

"Loser," my brother said with a fake cough.

"You better watch yourself, son," my father threatened from across the table.

"But, Dad, she really is a loser. She doesn't have any friends other than Michelle and all she does is sit in the house all day, which actually makes her a double loser," my brother stated.

"Okay, that's it, one more remark out of you and you'll be riding the bench at your next game," my father said while staring at my brother.

Before my brother apologized to me, he took a deep breath before rephrasing how I wasn't a loser and that I was just a little different.

"Different is good," said my father. "In my opinion, being different means that a person has a mind of their own and doesn't get easily influenced by their peers when trying to be someone or something they're not. So with that being said, SJ, maybe you should start being a little 'different' it may help your grades to improve." My father implied before heading into the kitchen, to scrape the remainders from his plate into the trash compactor.

"Hey babe! I forgot to tell you that Karla called for you this afternoon," my mother shouted from the dining room table.

"Did she say what it was regarding?" my father asked.

"Yes, she mentioned something about you stopping by her place to mount her new flat-screen television onto her living room wall," My mother stated.

"She can pay a professional to come in and mount it for her," my father responded.

"Honey, don't be like that. After all, she doesn't have anyone that can handle all of the manly duties around her place," my mother pleaded.

"Okay, I guess that I can go over and mount it for her," he replied while giving in to my mother's request.

"Well, at least sit down and eat your dessert before you take off," my mothered said.

"No, thank you! I'll pass on dessert. Besides, I'm too stuffed from the delicious meal that SJ and I put together for you all." He stated. But not even he, could contain his laughter being that my mother had already revealed how she had found the frozen entree boxes in the trash bin outdoors.

Chapter Twelve
BEAUTIFUL LIAR—PART 1

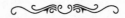

Once the gates opened to my aunt's condo, my father's BMW pulled up outside of her place. "Hello!" my father said while letting himself into the slightly dim house.

"I'm in here!" my aunt called out from the living room. When my father entered the room, he discovered that my aunt's new television had already been mounted onto her wall. "Don't mind the television. I paid the delivery crew to put it up for me," my aunt said.

"So why did you call me over, Karla? And what do you have on?" he asked as my aunt slowly uncrossed her exposed legs.

"I'm wearing the lingerie set that you bought for me," she replied while approaching my father.

"I told you that we could no longer see each other, especially after almost having our cover blown the other night at the restaurant," he replied angrily.

"Oh really?" my aunt asked.

"Yes, really," my father shot back.

"Please don't do this to me, daddy. I know that you're in love with my sister, but how do you expect for me to just walk away now? After all, I had you first."

"Karla, first of all, you never had me and secondly, we only screwed around once before you introduced me to Kelly," my father responded.

"You're right, and it'll break Kelly's little heart to know that you and I have been having an affair for the past year now," my aunt replied.

For one of the first times ever, my father was speechless. As he attempted to walk away from my aunt, she quickly grabbed ahold to one of his belt buckles and pulled him in towards her direction. When she finally had him where she wanted him, she attempted to seduce him by kissing on his neck.

"Karla, I can't do this," my father pleaded.

"Oh yeah! Well I think that your friend down below is thinking something else," she replied while pushing him down onto her leather, love seat. As he became quickly aroused, he tried to change the subject by asking where her children were.

"Give me a break, Steven. I'm not that careless and you should know by now that it's their father's week to have them" she replied.

"Well anyway, this is the last time and I mean it," my father stated before my aunt withdrew her robe to silence him.

Chapter Thirteen
BEAUTIFUL LIAR—PART 2

When Michelle and I heard the garage door slam, we nearly jumped out of our skins as my mother stormed past us and into the master bedroom.

"Kelly! What's going on?" he asked while trying to block most of the blows that she threw at him.

"How could you?" she asked while trying to catch her breath.

"How could I what?" he questioned, with a puzzled expression on his face.

"How could you have the audacity to lie down with my sister and think that for one second it would be okay for you to crawl back into the bed that we share?" she asked with tears in her eyes.

I nearly went into shock after hearing my mother's accusations towards my father. It just didn't seem like his character to do what she was accusing him of. That is, until I heard my mother say how humiliated she was when her doctor had mistaken her for my aunt and questioned if she and her partner, Mr. Haynes, had taken all of their prescriptions to cure their sexually transmitted disease for Gonorrhea.

Just the thought of it all made my mother gag as she went on to say how she had already put two and two together, that my father was possibly my aunt's 'mystery man'.

"Things are now starting to add up," my mother said while pacing around their room in circles. "First it was your late nights at the office. Then all of the awkward favors that she was requesting from you, not to mention the provocative dancing that she was doing when she danced with you at our anniversary party," my mother said at the top of her lungs.

"Baby, can we please talk about this?" my father pleaded while dodging some of the items that my mother had started to throw at him.

"Get the hell out of my house," she said as calmly as possible, while pointing towards their bedroom door.

Before Michelle and I could move away from the door in time, my father had caught the two of us eavesdropping on their conversation. But instead of scolding us, he did exactly as he was told and left out of the garage door.

CHAPTER FOURTEEN

MR. OFFICER

"Where are you headed to in such a hurry?" the police officer asked my mother as she scrambled around in her purse to retrieve her driver's license.

"My apologies, Officer. I was headed over to my parents' house to check on my ill father," my mother fibbed. The truth was that she was headed over to my aunt's place to get revenge. Because before she left the house, she informed me and Michelle that she had some unfinished business to take care of and that we were not allowed to mention the fight that she had with my father to no one, not even to my siblings.

"Okay, ma'am. Although I clocked you going fifty-five in a forty-mile-an-hour zone, I'm going to let you off this time with a warning on account of your father being ill," the officer said after running her license and registration.

"Oh, thank you, Officer! I'll promise to be more cautious of the speed limit," my mother said before continuing on her journey.

* * *

"Red, don't you think that you should check on your mother?" Michelle asked with concern. "Yes, but I'm too afraid to contact her. I've never seen her get so angry, let alone raise her voice," I replied.

"Well that's why they invented text messaging," Michelle said while handing me my phone.

* * *

Hi mom! I'm was just texting you to make sure that you were okay and to ask for you to hurry home bcus SJ, Raven and I all need you right now, more than ever. Plz call or txt me back once you read this mssg. Love you!!!

* * *

"Damn it!" my mother shouted after her low fuel light came on. Not wanting to chance running out of gas, she got off on the next exit. While waiting for her truck to fill up, my mother decided to scan through some of her missed text messages while avoiding all of the ones from my father. After she read my text message, she immediately broke down into tears as she thought about what her life would have been like if she hadn't gone against her father's wishes and married my father. But on the other hand, she had so much to be thankful for because throughout it all, she still had her three beautiful children back home, who were waiting for her return.

"Red's right! My children need me," she said to herself, before wiping the tears from her eyes and driving home.

Chapter Fifteen
SPIRITUAL HEALING

Over the next couple of weeks, I watched helplessly as my mother began to let herself go. It seemed as though on some days, that she would just roll out of bed, while neglecting to shower or comb her hair. But it wasn't until she had completely stopped going on her morning jogs that I knew she had officially hit rock bottom. My father's absence from the house was beginning to take a toll on everyone, including myself. While my brother's behavior and performance at school was starting to get out of control, my sister's bubbly personality however, was starting to become more diminished by the day. As for myself, I had become much lonelier now than ever before. Although I was far from a daddy's girl, I still missed having my old man around, just so he could ask me about my day or to compliment me on the days when I felt unpretty.

Before my family and I self-destructed, I decided to reach out to one of the closest people in our family, which was my Uncle Hank. Once he and his wife got word about my family's crisis, they immediately came to our rescue.

* * *

"Yes, they're here!" I said to myself after hearing the doorbell ring. When I opened the door, I found my Aunt Jenny and Uncle Hank standing in our doorway, holding several bags of groceries along with a box of my mother's favorite chocolates.

"Hey, sweetie! How's it going?" my uncle asked while giving me a peck on the cheek.

"I wish that I could say that things were improving, but anyway, thanks for coming," I replied.

"No need to thank us, Red. That's what family is for," he said before walking off toward my mother's room.

"So, how's school going?" my aunt asked as she and I was putting away the groceries that she and my uncle had brought over.

"School couldn't be any better!" I replied. But honestly, between trying to maintain my 4.0 grade-point average and getting Ian caught up on his homework, I was starting to become overwhelmed. I just couldn't find it in me to tell him that I could no longer do his homework because I really enjoyed his company.

"Hey, honey! Do you mind checking on Kelly for me?" my uncle asked as he joined me and my aunt back in the kitchen.

"Sure thing, just make sure that you both keep an eye on my green bean casserole," she said before walking out of the kitchen.

"Where's your brother and sister?" he asked.

"They both had practice but they should be coming in at any minute now," I replied.

"Ok, well look here Red, I want to thank you for reaching out to me, because I was starting to get really worried when your mother wasn't returning any of my phone calls or text messages," he stated. "Speaking of phone calls, have you heard from your father lately?"

"Yes, he calls every night to check on everyone, but whenever he tries to speak to my mother, she disconnects the call."

"Well, I can only image what you and your siblings are going through right now, but I want for you all to keep an open mind, that you all must forgive those who trespass against you because we're all human and no one is perfect." With that being said, I don't want you or your siblings holding on to any grudges towards your father or your aunt. Do you understand me?" he asked.

"Yes, sir," I replied.

Later that night, after my aunt and uncle ate dinner with me and my family, I couldn't help but to think about the conversation that he and I had earlier that day. How could he possibly expect for me—let alone my mother and siblings not to be angry at the two people who were responsible for breaking up our happy home?

Chapter Sixteen
SWEET DREAMS

~~~

"What is it now, Michelle?" I asked myself while retrieving my vibrating cell phone from off my nightstand. But to my surprise, it wasn't Michelle who was trying to get my attention. It was Ian instead.

Ian: *wyd

Me: Not too much, just finishing up some homework, what's up with you?

Ian: *Can you get out?

Me: Out???

Ian: *Yes, can you come outside? I'm almost on your street

Me: Sure, let me grab my jacket and I'll be right out

Ian: Ok

After reading Ian's text message, I immediately ran into the bathroom to freshen up. "I can't believe that I'm doing this and furthermore, how does he know where I live?" I asked myself as I continued to brush my teeth.

When it came to sneaking out of my parents' home, I had absolutely no clue as to what I was doing. But with my adrenaline pumping, there was no turning back now as I crept slowly down the stairs, past my parents' bedroom and out of the patio door.

"There you are! I was starting to think that you had reneged on me," Ian said as I climbed into the passenger side of his father's car.

"Oh, no, I would never do a thing like that," I replied.

"So, how was your day?" he asked.

"It was okay, other than my parent's still not being on speaking terms," I stated. Ian was fully aware of my family issues and by my father no longer being in the house and Michelle picking up extra hours at her job, I didn't have anyone else that I could vent to.

After conversing for over twenty minutes or so, Ian decided to thank me for helping him out with his lessons. Not wanting to rain on his parade, I decided not to mention how his extra homework assignments were starting to affect my own grades.

"Well, I'm not going to keep you up all night, I just wanted to tell you in person that I really appreciate everything that you do and I hope that things will work themselves out for you and your family's sake," he said before giving me a kiss goodnight on my cheek.

"You're more than welcome!" I replied while stumbling over my own two feet as I made my way back into my house. After making it quietly back up to my room, I opened an unread text message from Ian that read: "Sweet dreams!"

Chapter Seventeen
GIRL TALK

The following morning, I woke up to the sounds of laughter and falling pots. When I went downstairs to see who was keeping up all of the raucous, I found my father's mother, Ruth and my Aunt Lena in our kitchen, cooking up a big breakfast. "What time is it?" I asked while rubbing my eyes.

"Good morning, Red! It's time for you and your siblings to wash up for breakfast," my aunt replied.

Doing as I was told, I headed back upstairs to awaken my sister. "Raven, wash up for breakfast!" I shouted through her bedroom door.

"Okay, I'll be down in a few," she replied. Within minutes, we both joined our grandmother, mother, aunt and Michelle at the dinner table.

As usual, my grandmother and aunt had outdone themselves with the scrambled eggs, sausage links, pancakes, crepes, turkey bacon, and the fruit tray that they had prepared.

"Well, I'm glad that you two beauty queens could join us," my auntie said.

"Good morning, everyone" we both replied.

"Where's your brother?" my mother asked.

"His coach picked him up this morning for practice," Raven answered.

"So, how have my two favorite granddaughters been doing?" my grandmother asked.

"Grandma, we're your only granddaughters," Raven replied while laughing.

"Ahem," Michelle interrupted, while clearing her throat.

"I'm sorry, Michelle. Let me rephrase my question. How have all three of my favorite granddaughters been doing?" she asked as everyone laughed.

"Well, I thought that you'd never ask," Michelle said as she informed everyone about how much she hated her job. Being that Michelle was an only child, her parent's didn't put any pressure on her to work—that is until her father found out about her future plans to have a sex change with the allowances that he was giving her.

"Okay, is it my turn yet?" Raven asked, interrupting Michelle's mini tantrum.

"Sure," my mother replied.

"Okay, so I have my senior prom approaching in less than a month and I have yet to find a dress," my sister complained.

"I'm sorry, sweetie. It's my fault that I haven't taken the time out to take you shopping. It's just that with everything that's been going on, I just haven't had the time," my mother replied. "But I'll tell you what, how about we get together within the next couple of weeks to go shopping for you a dress," she said.

"Okay, that sounds good to me!" Raven anxiously replied.

"So, who's the lucky young man that will be escorting you?" my grandmother asked.

"My boyfriend of two years, of course," my sister replied.

"Well that's nice. He's a well-mannered young man," my grandma said.

"Well, last but certainly not least, what have you been up to, Red?" my aunt asked from across the table.

"Oh, not too much. I've just been a little busy with tutoring a classmate of mine and with job searching," I stated.

"Why are you job searching if you're making money tutoring?" my aunt asked.

"Well, because I'm not charging this particular classmate of mine," I replied.

"And would this classmate just so happen to be the son of Mark Chalmers?" my aunt asked.

"Yes, ma'am," I said while cutting my eyes at Michelle for sharing my secrets with her mother.

"Now you look here, Red. Those Chalmer men are no good," she said, pointing her finger from across the table.

"They're all sneaky, conniving …'and good looking'," my grandmother added.

"Yes, and good looking," my aunt said while agreeing with her mother. "But the point that I'm trying to make is that you *never* allow for anyone to use you. Do you understand me?" my aunt asked.

"Yes, ma'am," I replied while turning red in the face.

"So, Lena, speaking of no good men, how is that brother of yours doing?" my mother asked. While waiting for the "Ms. Know It All" of the family to reply, the entire room grew so quiet that one could literally hear a pin drop.

"Steven is doing just fine," she finally replied while covering up the truth about how he had gotten on her last nerve, by talking about how much he missed his wife and children.

"Oh really?" my mother asked, not believing a word that came out of her sister-in-law's mouth.

"Cut it out, you two," my grandmother intervened. "Look here, Kelly, not only did we come over to check on you and the kids, but we also came over to ask if you would be willing to sit down and talk to your husband. Now, I know that whatever goes on in your household is none of my business, but everyone knows how old fashioned I am when it comes to relationships. I'm not trying to justify the wrongdoing of my son, but what I want for the two of you to realize is that, at the end of the day, the only people that the two of you are hurting is your children. Kelly, you know that I love you like my very own, but I just want you to understand that marriage is about communication, compromising and learning from your mistakes," she said while walking over to comfort my mother, who was crying silently in her chair.

With all of the commotion that was taking place, no one heard our house phone ringing but Michelle. "Aunt Kelly, it's your brother," she said while handing my mother the phone. As my mother wiped the tears from her eyes, she then excused herself from the table so that she could have some privacy.

CHAPTER EIGHTEEN

FAMILY MEETING

Later that evening when all of our guests were gone, my mother called my siblings and me into her bedroom for a family meeting. "What's going on, Mom?" SJ impatiently asked.

"Everything is just fine, sweetie," she replied. "I just wanted to be the first to tell you all that after having a long conversation with your Uncle Hank today that he has finally convinced me to attend a marriage retreat/ counseling with your father."

"That's great, Mom! Now we can be a family again," Raven said while jumping for joy.

"Well, let's not get ahead of ourselves. Your father and I have so many things to address over the next couple of weeks of counseling, before we can determine whether or not if we'll be getting back together," my mother said.

"Well, Mom, regardless of the outcome, I just want to let you know that I'm proud of you for even taking the initiative to try to save your marriage," my sister said while initiating a group hug.

"Wait a minute, who's going to watch us while you're away?" my brother asked.

"Your grandparents will be staying over here with you all to keep the house in order," my mother replied before going through our house rules.

CHAPTER NINETEEN
THE MORE THE MERRIER

Nearly a month had gone by since my mother had last seen my father and if it wasn't for my uncle Hank calling in a favor to one of his good friends named, Dr. Boyd, my mother probably would have never even considered going to marriage counseling.

"Mr. Haynes, out of all of the women that you could have had an affair with, why your wife's sister?" the counselor asked halfway through my parents' first session.

Before answering the question, my father hesitated for a moment as my mother and Dr. Boyd both stared at him, anxiously waiting for an answer. "Well to be completely honest, Doc," he said before clearing his throat. "Before my wife and I met, I was a senior and also a ladies man at my college. Wherever there was a party, women and liquor, I was there.

"I met Karla at least six months prior to me meeting Kelly at a campus party and within that same night of meeting her, she and I had a one-night stand," my father confessed while avoiding any eye contact with my mother. "After that night, the two of us never saw each other again until the night of my graduation celebration from law school. That night, when she and I ran into each other again, she introduced me to Kelly. After I realized that the two of them were twins, I had planned on picking up where Karla and I had left off, but this time as a threesome," he stated.

Before my father could go any further with his story, my mother's composure had finally been broken-- causing for her to storm out of the room.

"Okay, let's take a ten-minute break," Dr. Boyd said to my father as he left the room to comfort my mother.

Not wanting to chance taking any more blows to the face, my father decided to stay behind. "What have you done?" he asked himself while covering his face to hide his shame.

"Mrs. Haynes, please try to calm down," Dr. Boyd instructed as my mother attempted to catch her breath.

"You don't understand," my mother said while gasping for air. "I sacrificed everything to be with that man." she said while pointing towards the room that my father was in. The slender man then assured her, that she would feel much better if she expressed to my father, how she was feeling rather than to keep it bottled up inside of her.

Shortly after finally convincing my mother to face my father again, Dr. Boyd poured the two of them a glass of water. "Mr. Haynes, whenever you're ready, you may proceed," the counselor instructed.

"Okay, but before I go any further, Kelly, I just want to let you know that I've never loved anyone the way that I love you!" my father said while staring into my mother's puffy eyes. As he continued on with his story, my father came clean about his affair with my aunt and how he would be willing to do anything to get his family back.

Chapter Twenty
VIDEO VIXEN

While my parents were away for counseling, my siblings and I were doing nearly everything that my mother had instructed for us not to do while she was away. My brother was staying up past his curfew, playing his video games while my sister gossiped the night away, talking on her cell phone. As for me, my late-night adventures with Ian had become more frequent as I slipped in and out of the house every night, while my grandparents were sound asleep.

"Come closer," Ian demanded while pulling me over to the driver's side.

It wasn't until Ian had begun to kiss on my neck, when I knew that I was asking for trouble. As he continued to plant gentle kisses amongst my flesh, I couldn't help but to quiver from butterflies that danced around in my stomach.

So this is what it feels like to be turned on? I thought to myself as my hormones and adrenaline had begun to take over my body.

In the midst of us engaging in foreplay, Ian's private area had begun to erect. Seeing how I was turning him on made me want to take it up a notch, so I decided to unbutton my blouse.

"Wow, nice racks!" he said while caressing them. "Do me a favor and grab a condom from out of the glove compartment," he instructed.

"But Ian, I ... I ... I'm not ready to have sex," I stated.

Prince Charming he was, let out a slight chuckle while he licked his lips. "So are you telling me that you're still a virgin?" he asked.

"Yes, I am," I replied shamefully, with my head down.

"There's nothing to be ashamed about, baby girl," he said while lifting my chin up and planting a soft kiss onto my lips.

"You can just give me a blow job instead," he suggested.

"But I've never …"

"Shush," he said while putting his finger up to my lips to silence my words. "Don't worry. I'll instruct you," he said, massaging the back of my neck.

Don't be such a baby. After all, all of your peers are doing it, so why not try it out? My subconscious mind sneered out. I then took a deep breath before closing my eyes and doing what Ian had instructed for me to do.

When the moment came for him to climax, I quickly rose up only to find him holding his cell phone in his hand.

"Were you recording me?" I frantically asked.

"Calm down, Trinity, it was only for like thirty seconds or so," he replied.

"But I didn't give you permission to do so," I shot back with an attitude.

"Relax, no one is going to see it and besides without my fingerprint, there would be no way possible for anyone to bypass my security code," he assured me before we said our goodbyes for the night.

* * *

After making my way back into the house that night, I tossed and turned in my bed with the fear of knowing that my reputation could be possibly ruined if Ian's phone ever got into the wrong hands.

CHAPTER TWENTY-ONE

SENORITA HAYNES

"Well, you look like crap," Michelle said as she joined me and Camilla for lunch in the ladies' room.

"Why, thank you!" I replied sarcastically.

"Let me guess, you pulled an all-nighter so that you could finish Ian's homework?" she teased.

"Actually, you're wrong. I'm tired because Ian and I lost track of the time last night when we were outside talking in his father's car," I replied with an attitude.

"You and Ian talking all night? I'm sorry, but I just don't see it," Michelle shot back.

"Well, you don't have to see it and besides, Ian has been the only shoulder that I've been able to cry on ever since my family's crisis," I stated before storming out of the ladies' room.

"Jeez, what's gotten into her?" Michelle asked, as she and Camilla stood there in shock from my sudden outburst.

* * *

That afternoon during my Spanish class, Camilla dropped a note on the top of my desk on her way over to the pencil sharpener. In the note, she inquired on if everything was okay between me and Ian being that he was sitting across the room from me. After replying that Ian and I were just fine, she picked the note back up on her way to her seat.

Although I was clueless as to what was really going on between the two of us, I had to play it cool because of my previous episode that I had in the ladies' room just moments before class had started.

But deep down inside, I was literally having a meltdown because Ian hadn't said two words to me during the entire class.

Not wanting to cause a scene or to keep staring at him from across the room, I decided to distract myself by drawing a couple of sketches in my art folder.

"Senorita Haynes, this is not an art class. Please but away your pencil and notepad," Mrs. Garcia said. "Oh! And by the way, I'd like to have a brief meeting with you after class."

"Ooh ..." my classmates all sounded as I flushed from embarrassment. I had never been more humiliated in my life and to make matters even worse, Ian shook his head at me, in disappointment from across the room.

When the dismissal bell had finally rung, Mrs. Garcia walked over to her classroom door to lower the shade on the window.

"I must be in big trouble." I said to myself as my teacher approached me.

"Ay yi yi, Senorita Haynes," Mrs. Garcia said as she sat down in her chair. "Have a seat." She instructed while nodding towards an empty chair that was located next to her desk. As I sat across from the short, gray-headed woman, I couldn't help but to stare at the large mole that protruded from the left side of her nostril. "What's going on with you?" she asked. "You were one of my tops students, but during the past few weeks, your grades have been mysteriously going downhill while Senor Chalmers' grade on the other hand, has been improving tremendously," she said with a disappointed look on her face. Feeling both ashamed and embarrassed, I informed her that I would do better. "Well I hope so, because you're a bright, young lady and I really don't want to see you get off track," she said while handing me a blue slip for my next class.

* * *

As I sat in the back of my art class, my conscience began to bother me as I thought about how disappointed my parents would be if they found out about my failing grade. "That's it! After today, I'm going to put my foot down and tell Ian that I will no longer be able to assist him with his assignments," I said to myself.

Chapter Twenty-Two
THE NEW GIRL

Once my art class was over, Michelle met me at my locker. "Are you okay?" she asked.

"Yes, I'm just a little tired, that's all," I replied.

"Well, I apologize if I offended you earlier today in the ladies' room," Michelle said.

"It's okay, I know that you didn't mean any harm," I replied. "Are you staying over today to help decorate the cafeteria for the mother and son dance?" I asked.

"Absolutely not. I just got my nails repainted in my cosmetology class," Michelle replied while holding her hands out in front of my face.

"Nice!" I replied while admiring her hot pink nails.

"I know, right! This color looks fab with my complexion," she added.

"Umm, who's that?" I asked while nodding towards the hallway ahead.

"Oh, that's Fallon Nelson, she's the new girl. Her and her family just moved here from Houston, Texas," she replied.

"And how do you know all of this?" I asked.

"Because she's one of my lab partners in my chemistry class," she answered. "Now, normally I would have found an excuse to kick her out of my all-male group, but she's different," Michelle said while gawking over her as she made her way down the hall. "If I were straight, I'd definitely ask her out on a date," he shared.

"T.M.I. Michelle and by the way, she's not that hot!" I jealously replied, while studying the girl's petite frame. *Who am I kidding?* I said to myself. She was so stunning that I couldn't take my eyes off of her. From her piercing blue eyes on down to her curvaceous body, she was everything that I was not. Not only did I envy her because of her looks but also because Ian was walking along the side of her, carrying her schoolbooks. Uncertain as to what had come over me at that moment, I slammed my locker door closed before storming off towards the cafeteria.

After all of the decorations had been put up for the dance, I gathered my belongings and made my way towards the student parking lot. While I was approaching my vehicle, I noticed that there was a tall silhouette leaning against my car. As I got closer to the pole light in the parking lot, I was able to recognize the individual by the initials on his school jacket.

"Hey! How's it going, Red?" Ian nervously asked.

"What's it to you?" I asked with an attitude.

"Well, I was asked because I wanted to treat you to the movies this weekend," he replied while staring deep into my eyes.

Unable to break away from his hypnotic gaze, I instantly forgot that I was ever mad at him. "This weekend?" I asked.

"Yes, this Sunday," he answered.

"A movie would be nice," I said while trying to keep my composure.

"Okay, cool! I'll text you with the show times on Sunday," he said before kissing me on the cheek and walking off towards his father's car.

"Okay," I whispered while watching him drive off from the parking lot.

Chapter Twenty-Three
EIGHT O' CLOCK ON THE DOT

Sunday couldn't have come fast enough as I anxiously waited for Ian's phone call. "So Red, what time is your date?" my mother asked while everyone was eating their Sunday dinner.

"Mom, it's not a date, we're just friends," I replied.

"Okay, okay, no need to get all defensive," she said.

"Well, who is this friend of yours?" my father asked from across the table.

"His name is Ian and he's Sheriff Chalmers' son," SJ said while butting into our conversation.

"Well thank you, Trinity, for sharing that information," my father sarcastically replied to my brother.

"Good job, Red. He's a hunk!" my mother said while winking an eye at me.

I then pleaded for everyone to change the subject, but my father continued on with his interrogation.

"So, what time will this Chalmers' guy be picking you up?" he asked.

"Dad! He's not picking me up and for the last time, it's not a date," I argued. "We're meeting up at the movie theater within the next hour or so to see *Hunger Games*," I replied.

"Okay, well, since it's not a date, you won't mind coming in at your regular curfew," he replied.

"But, Dad, what if he wants to grab something to eat afterwards?" I asked.

"Well, I suggest that the two of you eat something from the concession stand," he answered in a stern voice while adding that he wanted me in the house at eight o'clock and not a minute later.

I don't know what had gotten into my father. Ever since he and my mother had returned from their retreat, he wasn't the same. But I'm pretty sure that it had a lot to do with my mother making him sleep in the basement until she said otherwise.

Throughout that afternoon, I must have sent Ian over a dozen of text messages to confirm if we were still on for the movies, but he didn't reply to any of them. Too embarrassed to tell everyone that Ian was possibly going to stand me up, I pretended like there was something wrong with my phone just so I had an excuse to borrow my sister's.

"Let's see if I get a response from him now," I said to myself while texting Ian's phone. Just as I had expected, he replied within seconds of me asking what he was doing.

Ian: *Who is this?

Me: *It's Trinity from your Spanish class

Ian: *what's up? I was just about to call you

Me: * Are we still on for the movies or not?

Ian: *Yes, meet me at the movie theater on the south side in about an hour

Me: *Ok, I'll see you then

After Ian had officially confirmed our movie date, I decided to erase all of our recent text messages out of my sister's phone because I didn't want her to see how desperate I was for reaching out to him.

* * *

When I finally pulled into the overly crowded, movie theater's parking lot, I noticed that I had two unread text messages. The first was sent from Camilla, who asked for me to give her a call once I was free and the other was from my father, who had decided to extend my curfew for an additional hour.

"There you are!" Ian's said as I entered the movie theatre. "Come on, we're in gate four," he said while leading the way. As I walked closely behind him, I couldn't help but notice that he was wearing a pair of sweatpants and a T-shirt that read 'Stay Focused.' How could he possibly expect me to stay focused when his muscular arms were nearly busting out of his shirt?

"Where are my manners? Would you like anything from the concession stand?" he asked.

"Oh, sure, just some popcorn and a cherry icy please," I replied as we took our places in the back of the concession stand line.

As much as I tried to enjoy the movie, I couldn't help but to notice that Ian was narrating nearly every scene in the movie.

"So I take it that you've already seen this movie?" I asked.

"Oh no, I just remember seeing those parts in the previews," he replied.

When the movie was finally over, I suggested for the two of us to grab a bite to eat since my father had extended my curfew. But Ian quickly turned down my offer, stating that he had a test to study for.

"What's going on Ian? It seems like you've been avoiding me ever since you and I made out the other night in your father's car." I asked with concern.

"Everything is just fine. I've just had a lot on my mind, that's all" he replied.

"Well would you like to talk about it?" I asked.

"No, thanks! I have to get ready for school on tomorrow" he said.

"Okay, well thanks for treating me to a movie and I guess I'll see you tomorrow in class," I said.

"You're welcome! And before I forget, are you by any chance almost done with my history paper?" He asked.

"Yes, I'm almost finished with it," I replied while getting into my car.

"Okay, good! I'll see you tomorrow," he said before we went our separate ways.

Chapter Twenty-Four

MIDDLE CHILD SYNDROME

Mom: *Good morning Red! Unfortunately I won't be able to attend your friend's birthday party with you on today. I forgot that I promised to take your sister shopping for her prom dress but hopefully I can make it up to you on another day, Love Mom!

"Why am I not surprised?" I asked myself after reading my mother's text message. It was the day of Camilla's *quinceañara* and my mother had bailed out on me like always. Luckily, I had already invited Michelle as my backup plan being that I had gotten so use to my parents cancelling and rescheduling different events with me over the past years.

But the truth is, ever since my brother was born, I've suffered from a severe case of the Middle Child Syndrome. You see, after my father had finally gotten the son that he begged my mother for, I was no longer the baby of the family. While my mother catered to Raven's every need, I was often left out of the loop, which caused for me to be nothing but a shadow of my sister's reflection. Nearly everything that my sister had owned was always passed down to me—starting with her hand-me-downs to her dented, 2003 Honda Civic that was in perfect condition when she had first gotten it as a gift for her sweet sixteen birthday. Where I on the other hand, got a box of Proactiv along with my sister's beat up car for my sixteenth birthday. It definitely sucked being the middle child because, as usual, I was often left with no one to talk to other than Michelle.

Chapter Twenty-Five
FIESTA

It was a quarter til three when Michelle and I took our seats in the back of the packed chapel. "Someone please pinch me!" Michelle said as she looked around the sanctuary at some of the men that were dressed up in tuxedos.

"Shush, let's not forget about your boyfriend, Di Angelo," I said to Michelle under my breath.

"D-ang-a-who?" she replied while continuing to gawk at Camilla's guests.

When it was finally time for Camilla to enter the chapel, everyone stood to their feet to honor her presence. She looked absolutely amazing in her lavender dress, which was complemented by a tiara that sat on top of her long, dark locks. As she and her chamberlain made their way down the aisle, I snapped several pictures of them along with the others who were a part of her court.

After the Liturgy of the Eucharist had concluded, the priest then presented Camilla to her family, friends and to the other members from her community.

"Camilla's ceremony was beautiful and all, but I can't wait to kick off these heels so that I can put on my dancing shoes," Michelle said as we followed the others over to the reception hall.

When we entered the venue, everyone stood around snapping pictures of the colorful decorations and centerpieces that filled the entire room. "Wow! I wonder what her wedding's going to be like," I said while admiring the place.

After all of the guest had been seated and served their three coarse, Mexican dishes it was time for Camilla to cut into her three layered cake. As everyone gathered around her to snap pictures,

Camilla's mother then brought out a small doll for her to present to her younger sister named, Santana. While everyone was enjoying their delicious cake, we watched in awe as Camilla's father got down on one knee to change over her flat shoes in exchange for a pair of high heels.

"That is so sweet!" Michelle said as she and I both wiped tears from our eyes.

"Okay, everyone, ¡Vayamos *de fiesta!*" the DJ announced after Camilla and her chamberlain had completed their first dance.

"What did he say?" Michelle asked me.

"He said, 'Let's party!'" I yelled over the music while leading Michelle to the dance floor.

While Michelle and I danced the night away, I had forgotten about all of my problems back home. That is until Camilla pulled me to the side and dropped a major bomb on me.

"Are you sure it was him?" I asked again just to make sure what I was hearing was true.

"Yes, I saw Ian at the movies with the new girl, last weekend," she said once more. "That's why I asked for you to contact me as soon as you had the chance," Camilla stated.

That explains how he knew all of the parts to the movie, I said to myself after thanking Camilla for sharing the information with me. As much as I wanted to crawl under a rock and die, I had to play it cool in order to avoid hearing the words, "I told you so" from Michelle.

CHAPTER TWENTY-SIX
CHANGE OF HEART

"You two-timing sleaze ball!" I yelled as I threw Ian's history and Spanish books at him from across the room.

"Trinity! What's gotten into you?" he asked while dodging the books.

"You've gotten into me, that's what," I replied, while yelling at the top of my lungs. "Not to mention, that you've been using me this entire time to do your homework" I added. "Yeah that's right, I know about your little trip to the movies with the new girl. Is she the reason why you haven't been returning any of my phone calls or sitting by me in Spanish class?" I asked with tears in my eyes. "Ian, I love you! How could you do something like this to me?" I asked while immediately regretting that I had confessed my love for him.

"Is everything okay in there?" Mrs. Chalmers asked while knocking on Ian's bedroom door.

"Yes, Mother, everything is just fine," Ian said, before turning back to look at me.

"Love? Trinity, we barely even know each other," he replied. "And besides, you knew exactly what you were getting yourself into before you started to catch feelings," he said while showing me to the front door.

As I reached for the doorknob, I heard Ian call out to me.

"Yes?" I replied, hoping that he had a change of heart.

"I was wondering if you had my finished report with you," he said.

"Of course I do," I replied while retrieving the ten-page research paper from my backpack-- only to rip it up in front of his face.

"No ... what are you doing?" he asked while attempting to put the small pieces of paper back together.

"What I should have done a long time ago," I replied before walking out of the door.

Chapter Twenty-Seven

PROM QUEEN

"The weather is just perfect!" Raven said as she jumped up and down with joy. "Where's my phone? I have to call the twins, Morgan and Leah, to see what time our limo will be arriving," she asked while running back inside of the house to search for her phone. Being that it was my sister's last year of high school, my parents along with her friends' parents all chipped in to rent the teens an all-inclusive SUV limousine for their prom.

As much as I wanted to stick around to help my sister get dressed for her big day, I couldn't because I had to be back at the high school to help with the final decorations.

* * *

Once I approached the school's parking lot, my stomach nearly hit the floor as I thought about how Ian and the new girl would soon be walking into the gymnasium together as a couple. Although he and I hadn't spoken since our big argument, I was still kind of bitter about not being his prom date.

"Hi, Trinity!" A couple of juniors named, Cassie and Ginger said as they approached me.

"Hey!" I replied, forcing a fake smile.

"We just wanted to let you know that everything is pretty much all set up. The only things that are left to do, is to make sure that the foggers are working properly and to set all of the silverware out on each table." Ginger stated.

"Okay, I'll start on the silverware," I said.

After the doors to the school's entrance, opened up, the gymnasium started to fill up with prom students.

When my sister and her boyfriend had arrived, I asked Cassie to take a couple of pictures of us since I wasn't able to do so before I had left from my home.

"Where is he?" I asked myself, while looking up at the entrance to see if there were any signs of Ian. But unfortunately there wasn't, not until he and Fallon made their grand entrance at nearly an hour after the prom had started. As the two of them strutted their stuff around the gymnasium, everyone in the crowd, cheered them on.

I could have nearly died on the inside, as I watched from across the room as the others snapped multiple pictures of the two of them. "Well, at least it's not Farrah," I said to myself while watching the couple, head to the dance floor.

Farrah must have read my mind as she approached me from behind.

"I bet that you wished it was you on the dance floor with Ian right about now, don't you?" she asked with a smirk on her face.

"Actually, I do," I replied. "But I'd be willing to bet money that you wished it was you as well." I said in retaliation.

"Yeah, you may be right. But you see, the difference between me and you is that I'm not afraid to take what belongs to me," she said while brushing past me and heading to the dance floor to steal a dance with Ian.

As much as I despised Farrah, I had to give her props for being so brave and risqué. I wished that I had the guts to just walk up to Ian to demand a dance.

"Hey! Is everything okay?" my sister asked. "I saw Farrah talking to you, and I know how devious she can be at times," Raven said.

"Oh, no, everything's just fine!" I answered while forcing a smile.

"Well good!" she replied, before asking me to dance with Seth until she returned from the ladies' room.

* * *

Seth and I danced for at least three songs before Principal Conners came over the microphone to announce the prom king and queen.

"Ladies and gentlemen, I'm not going to be before you long, but I would like to take the time out to tell each of you how stunning you all look on tonight," she said as the crowd cheered her on. "Now without any further delays, your '2013' prom king and queen are ... Ian Chalmers and Raven Haynes!" she announced.

As Ian and Raven made their way up to the stage to be crowned, everyone in the crowd cheered them on. Just seeing my sister up on the stage brought tears to my eyes because from her beauty to her personality, she definitely deserved her title as the prom queen.

* * *

While lying in my bed that night, I couldn't help but to think about how remarkable Ian looked in his white and canary-yellow tux. *I wonder what he's doing right now.* I thought to myself, while trying to eliminate any thoughts of him making out with the new girl.

CHAPTER TWENTY-EIGHT
I'M SORRY

"Knock, knock," my mother said as she made her way into my bedroom. "Good morning sweetheart! It's Michael and he says that it's very important," she added while handing me the house phone.

"Mom, I'll do it," I said to her as she attempted to clean up my messy room.

"Okay, fine, but I want you up and dressed within the next hour for church," she replied before walking out of my room."

"Hello!" I finally said into the phone.

"Trinity, OMG! We have a problem," Michelle said frantically.

"What type of problem?" I asked while rising up in my bed.

"I really don't know how to say this but there was a video of you on Spirit Book performing oral sex on Ian," she replied as calmly as she could.

"There was a *what?*" I shouted through the phone.

Spirit Book was a social site that many of the students and teachers at my school used for tutoring sessions and to upload pictures and videos of our school events throughout the school year.

"I can't believe this is happening to me!" I said while pinching myself, hoping to wake up out of this nightmare. But unfortunately for me, my bad dream had turned into reality.

"Well, if it makes you feel any better, the video has been flagged and already taken down, but I'm not certain as to how many people actually watched it," Michelle stated.

After receiving the news, I immediately ran downstairs into my family's computer room so that I could confirm whether or not if the video had been taken down. After I had finally logged onto the social site, the words *slut*, *whore*, and *freak* all popped up under my profile. "Oh no!" I said into the receiver after reading the rest of the comments that were posted under my profile. "My family and I are going to have to move out of the state—better yet, out of the country!" I said while panicking.

"Red, please try to calm down," Michelle said.

"How do you expected for me to remain calm when my reputation is on the line?" I asked with an attitude.

"Maybe you should contact Ian to try to sort this entire mess out," she suggested.

"Forget contacting him. I'm going to stop over there as soon as my family and I get out of church," I replied.

"Trinity, why aren't you upstairs getting dressed for church?" my mother asked as she entered our computer room.

"Sorry mom, I was just checking on my homework assignments." I replied, while quickly powering off the computer. "Michelle, I'll call you later," I said before hanging up the phone.

Later that afternoon, when church was over, I decided to skip out on Sunday dinner with my family so that I could drive over to Ian's place to confront him. After completely losing my appetite and missing out on quality time spent with my family, all I could think about was the cruel comments and dirty looks that I had received earlier that morning, during the church service. I guess that more people had heard about the video than Michelle and I had expected.

When I finally pulled up outside of my destination, I couldn't help but to notice that Farrah's new car was sitting in the driveway.

I wonder what she's doing over here, I thought to myself, as I made my way up to the front door. But before I could wonder any longer, both Ian and Farrah appeared in the doorway—staring as though they had seen a ghost.

"Why are you here?" Farrah finally asked.

"Excuse me but Ian, may I have a word with you?" I asked while ignoring her question.

"Yeah, sure!" he replied before excusing himself from Farrah's presence. During the walk over to my car, he informed me that he already knew why I was there.

"How could you do this to me?" I asked while trying to fight back my tears.

"It wasn't me," he replied.

"Well, if it wasn't you, who else could it have been, that has the exact same thumbprint as you?" I asked with my arms folded.

"I don't know. After the prom, things got pretty wild and all I remember is waking up next to Farrah," he said, while stopping dead in his tracks.

"So are you telling me that Farrah is responsible for uploading the video of me onto Spirit Book?" I asked while rolling my eyes.

"I'm saying that I don't know how the video got out and that I'm sorry that this happened to you," he said while looking down at the ground.

"Sure you are and I'm pretty sure that the two of you have gotten a good laugh out of all of this," I said before getting into my car and driving off.

CHAPTER TWENTY-NINE
THE BIG MOVE

That night after receiving several, harassing prank calls and text messages, I decided to ask my parents if I could switch schools. But unfortunately, being that the school year was almost over, they both denied my request.

Afterwards, I debated in my room for hours about whether or not I should tell them the truth as to why I wanted to change schools. But I just couldn't work up enough courage to look them in their eyes and tell them about my inappropriate video. "There has to be another way out," I said to myself before my sister entered my room.

"Hey! Are you okay?" she asked while walking over to comfort me.

"No," I replied while bursting into tears.

"Don't cry, Red. Everything's going to be okay," she assured me.

"How can you be so certain?" I asked.

"Well because I'm going to speak with Principal Conners, first thing tomorrow on your behalf. That way she'll be able to punish anyone who played a role in leaking Ian's video." she stated.

"Really? You'd do that for me?" I asked.

"Of course I will, Trinity! You're my little sister," she replied before walking out of my room.

The following morning, I pretended to have a stomach ache so that I wouldn't have to face my peers at school.

"Try to get some rest, sweetie and by the way, I left a pot of soup on the stove for you," my mother said before she left out for work that morning.

Throughout that day, Michelle kept me posted on what all was being said around our school pertaining to the video. "So far so good!" She replied through a text message, but it wasn't until when

Raven had sent me a text message, that stated that our principle was going to be out of the office until the end of the week.

"I'm doomed!" I said to myself while dismissing any thoughts of letting the assistant principle get involved.

The next day after my stomach ache had mysteriously gone away, I noticed while I was approaching my locker that someone had stuck some stickers onto the front of my locker that spelled out the words "Cock Sucker." I immediately turned red in the face as my peers pointed and laughed at me. Too ashamed to attend the rest of my classes for that day, I decided to cowardly hideout in the bathroom stall instead because that's where I felt most safe and secure-- away from my peers.

"So, did you hear about the porn video that Raven's little sister made with Ian Chalmers and a couple of other guys from the football team?" a random girl asked.

"Yeah, I heard about it, but I didn't think it was true, being that she's so quiet and all," her friend replied.

"Well, you know what they say, it's the quiet one's that you have to watch out for," the girl replied back before the two of them made their way out of the ladies' room.

"Trinity, are you in here?" Camilla asked as she and Michelle joined me in the restroom moments later.

"Yes, I am. Now please go away. I don't feel like talking," I replied.

"Red, we're not going anywhere, so you might as well come on out so that we can talk," Michelle demanded.

"You guys, please! I can't stand to look at myself right now, let alone anyone else," I pleaded.

"Trinity, we're not going to look down on you or judge you. Just please come out and talk to us," Camilla begged.

"No, I really don't feel like talking right now but I promise that I'll call you both later on tonight," I said before they finally decided to let me be.

CHAPTER THIRTY
GO LONG

Keeping my promise to Camilla and Michelle, I called them both that night to apologize for my behavior earlier that day. Being that they were my only support system besides my sister, they both accepted my apology.

After giving both of them my word that I would attend school on tomorrow, I decided to set my school clothes out for the next school day. But once again, after returning to school, the verbal sticks and stones that my peers threw at me were too much to bear, causing for me to retreat back into the restroom stalls.

Before the lunch bell sounded, I decided to head to the cafeteria like normal to grab something to eat. But to my surprise, when I entered the cafeteria, I found Farrah and a group of her friends already standing in the lunch line.

"Can this day get any worse?" I asked myself while turning away to avoid the crowd.

"Hey Trinity! Come here for a second," Farrah said while motioning for me to join her and her friends.

Not knowing exactly what I was getting myself into, I walked up to the crowd slowly to see what Farrah had wanted with me. "What's up?" I asked nervously.

"Oh, nothing much. I just wanted to let bygones be bygones and to give you my sincerest apology for leaking your PG-13 sex tape," she said, as her and a couple of her friends chuckled amongst themselves.

I could have kicked my own behind for thinking even once that she was going to be the bigger person by truly apologizing to me for what she had done. But after all, this was Farrah Cummings who

I was referring to, so I knew that an apology from her would never happen.

After being humiliated in front of the large crowd, I decided to head back to my comfort zone. That is, until one of the guys from the football team lounged a banana at me while yelling out for me to "go long."

"That does it! I can't take it anymore," I said to myself after the banana had hit me across my face.

CHAPTER THIRTY-ONE
BOTTLES UP

After storming out of the school building and arriving to my empty home, I decided to take a couple of my mother's sleeping pills, to help numb my pain. But after sitting in the dim bathroom for nearly an hour, I thought about how much easier life would be if I had just disappeared for good.

"No One Loves You, Not Even You"

As my reflection appeared abstract from the shattered glass,
My mind continued to fill with impure thoughts
That I prayed would shaken my troubles for good this time.

After taking a deep breath
To release some of the tension that had me captured,
I couldn't help but to think about ...
How I'm here but never seen,
How I spoke to deafened ears it seemed.

You see, I just wanted for another to notice me,
To make me feel here ... Alive,
But I had to remind myself that I was my own worst critic
Because she, they, them said it first,
Brought slight flaws to my attention, until I hated me.
I mean, I used to love me, every inch, curve, and flaw in my DNA
that made me.

Suppressed in my hand awaited the sixteen pills
That I had specially counted for every year that I've lived this
miserable life.
With tears flowing down both cheeks,
I watched in total shock, as the streams of blood raced down my
freshly opened wrist.

"Just get on with it,"
My sub-conscious finally sneered out at me.
"No one loves you, not even you ..."

CHAPTER THIRTY-TWO
REMAIN CALM

"Hello! Is there anyone home?" Michelle asked while entering through the unlocked, front door. "Poor Trinity. She must of been extremely exhausted for her to have left her keys in the door," Michelle said while removing the set of keys. After climbing to the top of the stairs, she noticed that there was a trail of blood that led from the bathroom into my bedroom.

"Oh my!" She gasped while running over to my unconscious body. My skin was much paler than usual and my body was very cold. Without any further hesitation, Michelle's shaking fingers, immediately dialed 911.

While waiting for the dispatcher to pick up, she stumbled across a dull razor along with an empty bottle of sleeping pills that lied next to my bed. Moments after providing the emergency operator with as much information as possible, she then proceeded to follow the safety procedures that the dispatcher had instructed for her to do in order to possibly save my life. "Red, please wake up," Michelle cried out as she wrapped a towel tightly around my wrist to stop the bleeding. When the paramedics had finally arrived, they discovered that I had a weak pulse and immediately rushed me over to the hospital.

After waiting patiently for several hours in the waiting room, my family along with Camilla were starting to become restless. That is until Dr. Tynes came out from the back to speak with my parents in private, regarding my failed suicide attempt.

"How is she doing, Doc?" my father asked.

"Well, she's doing much better thanks to that fine young man over there," the doctor replied, while nodding towards Michelle.

"If it hadn't been for his heroic actions, your daughter would have possibly bled to death," he stated. "My team and I did however, had to pump her stomach and put sixteen stitches in her left wrist." He said while also informing my parents about how lucky I was to be alive, being that I had just barely missed the main artery in my wrist.

"When can we see her?" my mother asked with tears in her eyes.

"Well, right now she's being transported into a recovery room, but after the nurses gets everything set up, I'll send someone out to get you all." The doctor said before walking off.

CHAPTER THIRTY-THREE

WELCOME BACK

After finally coming to, I woke up in my hospital bed, surrounded by my loved ones. My body felt very weak as I attempted to sit up in the bed.

"She's up, She's up!" my mother shouted out in excitement as she and my father rushed over to comfort me.

"Hey there, beautiful!" my father said while planting a kiss on my forehead.

"How are you feeling, sweetie?" my mother asked while looking down at the stitches in my wrist. Being that I was still feeling a little drowsy from all of the pain medicine, I was unable to answer any of my parent's questions. Which couldn't have been at a better time since I was feeling ashamed for all that I had put them through.

* * *

While one of the nurses was checking my vitals, my mother had decided to rejoin me in the room, after she had been previously escorted out by my father. After she had completely regrouped, she shared with me, how she and the family had to practically beg for Michelle to go home and get some rest, because she had refused to leave my side. She then went on to inform me that in a couple of days, I would be transported to a nice facility by a couple of nice doctors, before I was able to come home.

Even though I had been unconscious for a couple of days, according to my mother, I was far from stupid. I knew that the "nice doctors" that she spoke of were probably nurses who worked over at the Savannah Mental Institution.

"By the way, here's some Jell-O and crackers to put in your stomach," she said while placing the food tray onto my lap.

"Thank you," I said to my mother who was doing nearly everything possible for me not to see the tears in her eyes.

"Knock, knock," a familiar voice said before opening my privacy curtain.

"Hi, Michelle!" I responded in a low tone.

"Welcome back!" she said while walking over towards my hospital bed. "How are you feeling?" she asked after my mother had excused herself from the room, to give us some privacy.

"I feel like crap," I replied.

"Well at least you don't look like it," she stated, before informing me how she had braided my hair while I was unconscientious.

"Thanks!" I said while reaching up to stroke my bushy braids.

"You're welcome! And these are for you," Michelle said while placing the teddy bear and flowers that she and De Angelo had bought for me across the room with the rest of the cards and balloons that filled my room.

"Wow! Where did all of that come from?" I asked feeling slightly overwhelmed.

"From different ones, such as your family, Camilla, your church members and some of the staff members at the school," Michelle replied.

There was an awkward moment of silence before I decided to ask Michelle about how I had ended up at the hospital. But after she had informed me that it was her who had saved my life, all I could do was cry.

"Don't you ever scare me like that again," she said while wiping tears from her eyes.

As much as I regretted what I had done, the only thing that I could do to make things right, was to apologize to Michelle and also my family for trying to take the cowardly way out.

* * *

During my recovery at the hospital, I had several visitors who stopped in to check on me, including my aunt Karla. It was definitely awkward seeing her under these circumstances, being that she and I hadn't seen each since my parents' anniversary dinner.

"Hello, Red! My aunt said as she and an older woman entered the room. "I would like for you to meet your Grandmother Martha" she said while extending her hand out towards the woman.

"It's a pleasure to finally meet you!" the redheaded woman said with a slight grin.

I couldn't believe my eyes as I continued to stare at the women like a deer in headlights. I don't know if I was more excited that she had come to visit me or if I was just happy to have finally found someone in my family, who I strongly resembled.

While I was still trying to grasp the idea of me meeting my grandmother in person, my aunt informed me that she and my mother were back on speaking terms.

"Really?" I asked.

"Yes, she's the one who told me that you were in the hospital" my aunt stated before informing me about their reconciliation brunch, that was put together by my Uncle Hank.

After my visiting hours was over, I made my aunt and grandmother both promise that they would keep in touch with me.

CHAPTER THIRTY-FOUR
THE VERDICT

Before I was transported to the Savannah Mental Institution, I was introduced to a lady detective by the name of Annette Roseburgh. After getting acquainted with the slender women, she informed me that she needed to ask me a few questions pertaining to my incident. After answering all of her questions to the best of my ability, she got a little annoyed with me once I refused to give up the names of my peers that played a role in my harassment. Although I knew what my peers had done was wrong, I didn't want to be labeled around the town or at my school as a rat or a snitch.

But unfortunately, Detective Roseburgh didn't need my permission to confiscate my cell phone along with my family's home computer being that my parents had already took it amongst themselves to press charges against all of the individuals who were involved with my cyberbullying attack.

While the detective and Principal Conners both worked hard on their investigations, my parents decided that it would be best for me not to attend school for the rest of the school year; with the exception of Michelle and Camilla taking turns to help me get caught up on all of my missed assignments.

Since my incident, I had lost all contact with Ian, up until a couple of days before our court appearance when he had decided to send a bouquet of yellow roses to my home. Inside of the arrangements, I found a small card which read:

Sorry for all of the pain and confusion that I've caused you and your family.

Sincerely, I.C.

After my father found out about the flowers, he immediately tossed them into the trash.

"I don't want you to socialize or to speak to him ever again. Do I make myself clear?" my father asked in a stern tone.

"Yes, sir." I shamefully replied. But I knew that it wasn't me who he was mad at. It turns out that Mr. Chalmers had approached him earlier that week, in attempt to bribe him with a check if he dropped the charges against his son. Which later resulted in my father physically tossing him out of his law firm, after he had informed Mr. Chalmers that there wasn't enough money in the world that could amount up to any of his children's lives.

On the day of the reading of the verdict, there was a lot of tension built up between the families in the court and the auditorium being that all of the cases and hearings were taking place in the very same day. But regardless if we were ready or not-- it was time for the verdicts to be read.

"In the case of Ian Chalmers versus the Savannah School Board of Education, we have come to the conclusion to suspend you for the remainder of the school year. You will, however, still be able to graduate by receiving your diploma by mail," one of the school officials announced.

Things could have been much worser for Ian but being that he wasn't the initiator who uploaded the video of me onto Spirit book, suspension was the school's only course of action. But as far as the judge's punishment for him, he was put on probation for a year while also being ordered to attend six anti-bulling classes before his twelve months of probation had expired.

"In the case of Farrah Cummings versus the Savannah School Board of Education, we have reached a unanimous decision of expulsion, for a total of twelve months. Being that you were in violation of the no bullying policy and also because you were the initiator of the cyber prank that nearly caused one of your peers to end her life." The school board official said before informing her that all of her belongings from her locker would be packed up and sent to her in the mail.

Hours later, when it came time for the judge to read the verdict for Farrah, he didn't show any signs remorse for her. "Miss Cummings, I can honestly say that you are nothing but an insecure coward who gets a kick out of targeting and harassing harmless individuals whom you know will never stand up to you." The judge said while leaving nearly everyone in the courtroom speechless. Although his words may have seemed harsh, he couldn't help but to sympathize with me and my family, being that he had gotten so fed up with the increasing number of teen deaths trials that were predominately caused by cyberbullying.

After everything was all said and done, Farrah's mouthy attitude had gotten her up to two years of probation and also six anti-bullying classes that she had to have completed before she could register for school the following year.

As far as for the other students that played a part in my harassment, they too were suspended for the last two weeks of the school year and had to complete the six step, anti-bullying program, before they were allowed to sign up for school that fall.

EPILOGUE

Being that tomorrow is never promised, my family and I are all learning how to take things one day at a time. That way, we'll be able to live, laugh and love one another a little more before the time comes for me to venture off on my own, into this cold world-- that has no remorse, limits or mercy for its actions.

But luckily, as of today, I am able to walk through the hallways at my school with my head held high because I can proudly say, that I am a survivor of cyberbullying.

"The Red Rose"

Like the beautiful, delicate flower, I am a rose ...
Roses are red, violets are blue,
I am a survivor of cyber-bullying.
What about you?

It is now my season
For me to blossom through
The fractures in the concrete
That once kept me cold, isolated and lonely.

That is until, I was awaken
By a kiss from the sun
And the tears from the raindrops,
That I was able to emerge
Through my darkest pain
Into a beautiful, delicate flower called a Rose.

ENOUGH ALREADY!

If you or anyone that you know is currently suffering from any form of bullying or are having any thoughts of suicide, please seek help from the free and confidential source listed down below.

1) **National Suicide Prevention Lifeline:** phone# 1-800-273-TALK (8255)

ABOUT THE AUTHOR

Jade Marie is a new, upcoming writer who delivers an exceptional first novel titled "A girl called Red." In this highly anticipated novel, she uses her creative writing skills and broad imagination to connect with her readers mentally and emotionally. She resides in Benton Harbor, Michigan along with her son and is hard at work on her next novel. Visit her at www.missjademarie.com